DISCARD

The Golden Age of the Galleon

The Golden Age of the
GALLEON

FRANK KNIGHT

COLLINS
St James's Place, London

William Collins Sons & Co Ltd
London · Glasgow · Sydney · Auckland
Toronto · Johannesburg

First published 1976
© Frank Knight 1976

ISBN 0 00 195290 0

Set in Monophoto Bembo by Tradespools Ltd, Frome, Somerset
Made and Printed in Great Britain by
William Collins Sons & Co Ltd Glasgow

Contents

1 *The Galleons at Cadiz*   *9*
How Drake with the new English galleons "singed the king of
Spain's beard".

2 *Trouble Brewing*   *21*
The beginnings of the quarrel. Philip II's ambitions. English
merchants and seamen and their desire for trade.

3 *The Traders*   *30*
The three voyages of John Hawkins. Spanish treachery at San
Juan de Ulua.

4 *The Undeclared War*   *42*
The seamen take their revenge. Pirates and privateers. Drake's
raid on Panama and his voyage round the world.

5 *Ships and Sea Ways*   *53*
How the ships were navigated and manned.

6 *Towards War*   *64*
Preparations in England. Hawkins re-organises the navy. The
new galleons. Spain seizes English ships and Drake retaliates. The
Armada sails.

7 *The Armada Comes*   *73*
The Armada arrives in the Channel. The fire-ships at Calais. The
battle in the North Sea and the final scattering. "God breathed."

8 *The Sunset Years*   *82*
Aftermath of the Armada. Deaths of Frobisher, Hawkins and
Drake. The death of Elizabeth and the making of peace. The navy
dismantled.

Acknowledgements   *94*

Index   *95*

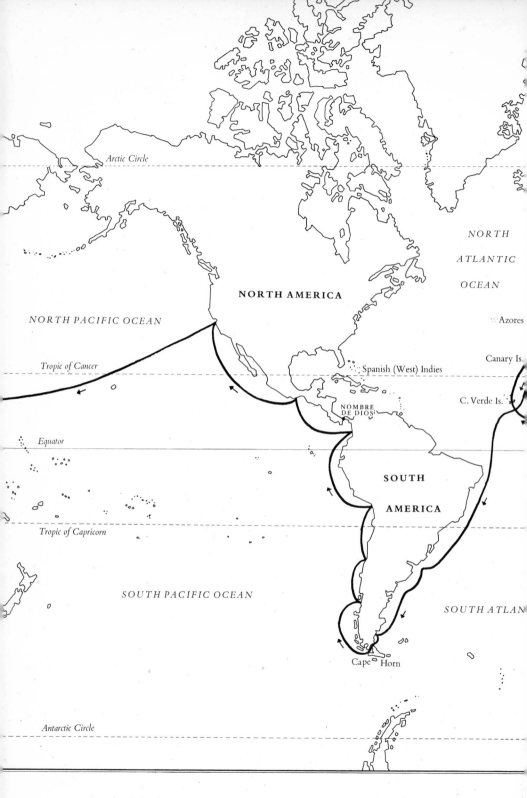

Arctic Circle

NORTH
ATLANTIC
OCEAN

NORTH AMERICA

NORTH PACIFIC OCEAN

Azores

Tropic of Cancer

Spanish (West) Indies

Canary Is.

NOMBRE
DE DIOS

C. Verde Is.

Equator

SOUTH

AMERICA

Tropic of Capricorn

SOUTH PACIFIC OCEAN

SOUTH ATLAN

Cape Horn

Antarctic Circle

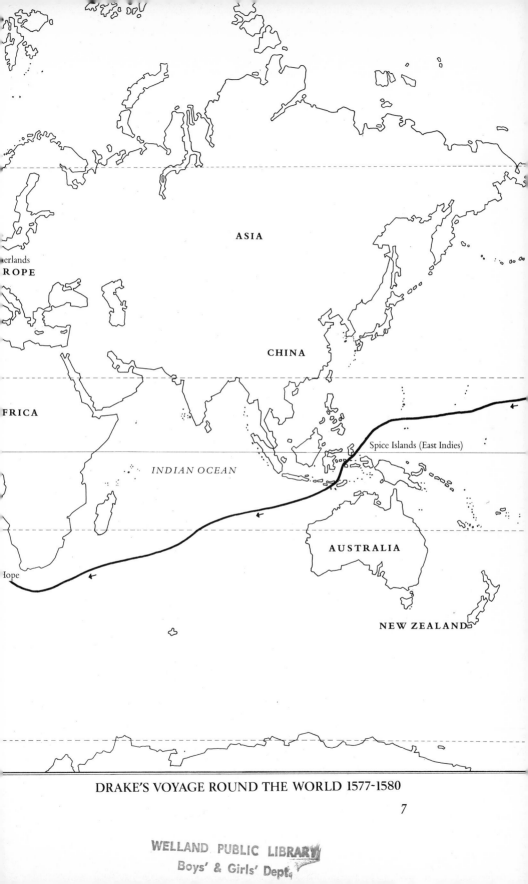

ASIA

erlands
ROPE

CHINA

FRICA

Spice Islands (East Indies)

INDIAN OCEAN

AUSTRALIA

Iope

NEW ZEALAND

DRAKE'S VOYAGE ROUND THE WORLD 1577-1580

1

The Galleons at Cadiz

In the spring of 1587 the sun of Spain was shining gloriously. It shone upon the steel helmets and breastplates of her soldiers as they marched across Europe. It shone upon the shiploads of gold and silver which came from the New World to pay for those soldiers.

Spain was the richest and most powerful nation in Europe. Her armies seemed unbeatable. They could boast of a score of victories in France and Italy; they had driven the Moors out of Spain and defeated them in Africa; they had stopped the Turks in their drive to conquer all the eastern Mediterranean.

Spain's empire was greater than Rome's had ever been. In Europe it included Portugal and parts of France, Italy and Austria, with most of the Netherlands. It covered almost all South and Central America and parts of what is now the United States. It had spread across the Pacific Ocean to include the Philippine Islands; and the union with Portugal had brought it settlements in India, the East Indies, Arabia and Africa.

Yet Spain's ambition was not satisfied. She wanted to add England to her possessions in Europe. Occupation of England would give her a springboard for an attack on France, her old enemy; it would also make safe the passage of Spanish ships and troops to the Netherlands.

More than thirty years earlier Philip II of Spain had tried to win England by marrying its queen, Mary Tudor. The

Philip II of Spain had tried to win England by marrying
Mary Tudor. It had been a highly unpopular marriage
and after Mary's death and Elizabeth I's accession,
Philip sought revenge by planning an invasion.

attempt had not been successful. The English people had
refused to consider themselves Philip's subjects. They had
insulted him and his officers. Then Mary had died and the
English had chosen her sister Elizabeth to rule them, completely ignoring Philip's claim. Worse, they had restored the
Protestant religion which Philip and Mary between them had
abolished and which Philip hated.

There were other annoying matters. Elizabeth had helped

Mary Tudor's marriage to Philip II of Spain was not a
success. She alienated her people by enforcing the Roman
Catholic faith, and they refused to consider themselves
Philip's subjects.

Philip's subjects in Holland to rebel against him. She had
allowed Dutch and French pirates, who raided Spanish
shipping in the Channel, to shelter in English ports. She had
done almost nothing to stop English pirates from joining in
that game too. She had even encouraged English pirates like
Drake and Hawkins to attack Spanish colonies in the New
World, lending them ships and investing money in their
enterprises.

A sixteenth century Dutch warship. Elizabeth I assisted the Dutch in their rebellion against Spanish rule in the Netherlands.

13

For years King Philip had dreamed of punishing England for these crimes. Now, in the year 1587, he was ready to do it – or almost ready. In ports like Lisbon and Cadiz the ships were assembling; warships and supply ships, great carracks and slim galleasses, pinnaces and despatch boats and fat-bellied "hulks" bulging with stores, all to make up the greatest war-fleet the world had ever known.

Hundreds of new-made guns were being shipped from Italian iron-foundries. Ropes, spare masts and spars, tar and oil, salt meat, dried fish, biscuits, peas and beans and flour, gunpowder, barrel staves and iron hoops – the unending flood of stores of all kinds crowded the quays and warehouses and filled ship after ship in the harbours. Soldiers, recalled from distant garrisons, were gathering by the thousand. Far away in Belgium another army was being prepared to be shipped across the North Sea into England when the mighty armada should arrive.

This was to be the summer of victory. Nothing, in King Philip's view, could prevent it or even delay it. The Enterprise of England, as he had called the venture, *must* succeed, and *now*..

That must also have been the view of the citizens of Cadiz, where about half the great armada was being prepared. The harbour was one mass of shipping. Thousands of shipwrights, carpenters, riggers, armourers and stevedores were working furiously. The town was full of soldiers and sailors. Camps sprawled about the countryside for miles. Nothing could be thought of in Cadiz but the Enterprise of England.

Then on April 19 something occurred which did at least set the citizens of Cadiz staring seaward. A fleet of nine big ships, with smaller vessels in attendance, appeared off the port. A buzz of excitement, mingled with exclamations of incredulity, must have been heard on the quays, when word went round that they were flying the English flag. English ships, here at Cadiz? But why? And what impertinence!

Few people could have thought of danger, or even of the

*Model of an English galleon. Drake used the new
galleon, which was easily manoeuvrable in his attack
on Cadiz.*

possibility of an attack. Cadiz was an enormously strong
port. Its harbour was protected from seawards by a long
spit of land projecting five miles to the north-west, parallel
with the coast. On the inner end of the spit were several
powerful forts. Within the harbour itself was a fleet of
rowing galleys, carrying guns and soldiers, specially main-
tained for the defence of the port.

The citizens of Cadiz well knew how difficult it was for
big sailing ships to manoeuvre inside that protecting strip
of land. Their own ships sometimes had to be towed or
warped into or out of the harbour, and sometimes came to
grief. So what chance would an enemy ship have? It would be
a sitting target for the forts to shoot to pieces. Nobody but
a madman would attempt such an attack!

Nobody but a madman. Well, there were men who said
Francis Drake was mad. He had been mad when, fifteen years
earlier, he had set out with a handful of men and boys to
assault the Spanish treasure port of Nombre de Dios on the
isthmus of Panama. He had been mad to venture into the

15

Pacific Ocean with one tiny ship, the *Golden Hind*, to raid Spain's most distant colonies, and even madder to attempt to return home with his booty by sailing right round the world. He was mad now to think of sailing into Cadiz. His second-in-command, Admiral William Borough, told him so. But Drake ignored him as he had ignored men who had called him mad on those other occasions. "Then what do you want me to do?" poor Borough asked, and Drake replied curtly, "Follow the flagship."

Of course Drake was not mad. He took risks which to other men seemed crazy; but with Drake they were calculated risks. He knew the dangers, but he also knew the possibility of overcoming them. He knew his own powers – and he was probably the finest seaman of the age. He knew his men. Above all he knew his ships. And this time he knew that at least four of his ships were capable of doing all that he was about to ask of them. For they were the Queen's new galleons; the flagship *Elizabeth Bonaventure,* the *Lion* under William Borough, the *Dreadnought* and *Rainbow*.

Drake had already sailed the *Elizabeth Bonaventure* to the West Indies. He knew her capabilities exactly. He knew that she was faster, handier, and a better fighting machine than any older ship in the Queen's service or in the navy of Spain. This he was now determined to demonstrate to the Spaniards in their own territory.

So the people of Cadiz watched with amazement the English ships sailing in behind the spit. On they sailed, right into the outer harbour. Then they dropped anchor and opened fire. At almost point blank range their shot tore into the packed Spanish shipping. Scarcely a ball could miss a target of some sort. Within minutes one of the biggest ships of all, a huge 1,000 ton carrack, was on fire and sinking.

Amazement gave way to panic. In all directions cables were cut as crews tried frantically to move their ships out of range, into the inner harbour or even on to the beach. Drifting ships collided with each other. Some sank, some caught

Sir Francis Drake's daring exploit, "the singeing of the King of Spain's beard", crippled Philip II's Armada, and gave England time to assemble her own fleet.

On the map, the following labels are visible:

IRELAND•

ENGLAND•

FLAND

THE

COASTE

OF

FRANCE•

THE COAST OF SPAINE

*A contemporary sea chart showing the waters between
England, Spain, France and Flanders, through which the
Armada fleet sailed on its way to invade Britain.*

fire and set fire to their neighbours. Some were hit by the
guns of the forts, which seemed to be firing indiscriminately
into the mass.

In the midst of all this the harbour-defence galleys were
trying to get out, with swearing boatswains lashing the bare
backs of the slaves at the oars. But they had been moored in
the inner harbour. Now they had to fight their way out
through the chaos of shipping in front of them.

In theory in such confined waters oared galleys, able to
dash to and fro without regard to the wind, had every
advantage over big sailing ships. They could dart in and
attack and dart away again; or they could run alongside so
that their hundreds of soldiers could swarm over the sides of
the helpless galleons. There were many people ashore who

expected this to happen. Drake, they said, had brought his ships into a trap.

But it was not to be like that. When the galleys did at last get within range the English guns turned on them with deadly accuracy. As one seaman put it, the galleys were brushed away like flies. One sank and the rest fled. The English seamen-gunners returned to their main job.

All that day they did very much as they pleased, sinking, burning, capturing, transferring Spanish cargoes to their own holds. "Before night we had taken thirty of the said ships," one man remembered. "Five of them were great ships of Biscay, whereof four we burnt, the fifth being laden with iron spikes, nails, iron hoops, horse-shoes and other necessaries. Moreover we took three flyboats laden with biscuit. Likewise we burnt ten ships laden with wine, raisins, figs, oils, wheat and suchlike." But a cargo of choice wines intended for King Philip's own table was transferred into an English storeship.

That night the town and harbour were lit by the flames of burning ships. But the flames also showed the English galleons to the gunners ashore. "We had little ease," our seaman recalled, for guns from the forts were dragged along the beach to better positions, while at the same time the galleys attacked again. And then the Spaniards sent fireships drifting down upon the galleons.

Yet little damage was done. The shots from the shore still missed or fell short. The galleys dared not venture in too close. The fireships drifted past or were towed clear by English boats.

At first light in the morning the *Elizabeth Bonaventure* was seen to be lifting her anchor and hoisting sails. Was Drake about to try to work his ships out against the morning breeze off the sea? A hopeless task!

But he was not. To the horror of his second-in-command Drake was steering the flagship straight for the inner harbour. William Borough leapt into a boat and had himself rowed to the *Elizabeth Bonaventure* to protest. There was a little breeze now, but what if it died away altogether? It so often did in the afternoon, as Borough well knew.

He was too late with his protest. When he reached the flagship and called for Drake, an officer pointed laconically to the inner harbour. Drake had gone in with his men in the ship's boats. For Borough that was the last straw. He returned to the *Lion* and began to work her out to sea. He would see to it that at least one of the Queen's new galleons should be returned to her safely! For that act of mutiny Borough was later tried by court-martial and condemned to death, but the Queen intervened and saved him from the final penalty. He was a good officer and had served his country well. He was not the only man for whom Drake's dashing ways were beyond stomaching.

To most of Drake's men that raid into the inner harbour was pure joy. All day they boarded, looted, burnt and sank. For them the crowning moment came when they destroyed what may have been the biggest ship in the world at that time, a mighty carrack of 1,500 tons belonging to Spain's high admiral, the Marquis of Santa Cruz.

Then at last, late in the afternoon, Drake called his men off and the galleons were turned seawards. But now, as Borough had foretold, the breeze had faded almost to nothing. And promptly the galleys came out once more to harry them, thinking their chance had come. But yet again they found the fire of the English ships too much for them. Try as they might, they could not get close enough for their own smaller guns to be effective. As to running alongside so that their soldiers could board the galleons, that was quite impossible.

For an hour or two it was stalemate. The galleons could not move because there was no wind. They even had to drop their anchors to avoid drifting on to the beach. But neither the Spanish galleys nor the shore-based guns could do more than annoy them.

And then, with nightfall, Drake's renowned luck came to

the rescue. Or was it more than luck? Was it perhaps his seaman's instinct, or the result of his deep knowledge of inshore navigation and local conditions? At any rate it came – a breeze from the south-west. Anchors were raised, sails filled and were close-hauled. The galleons sailed out and left the Spaniards to survey the ruins of half an armada which should have sailed for England that summer.

Of course it would not altogether stop the Enterprise of England. The damage could be repaired, the ships and stores replaced; but not in that year. And another year would give England that much more time to prepare, to build and equip more of the terrible new galleons.

Drake made light of the affair when he called it "singeing the king of Spain's beard", but there was more to it than that. For one thing, the nations had been shown that Spain was not almighty. The Dutch had already shown that rebellion against Spain's dominion could be successful. Now the English, another relatively poor and unregarded nation, had carried war into Spain itself with spectacular success. Never again, perhaps, would Spain be held in such awe as she had been before.

Never again, either, would the oared war-galley be thought supreme. "We now have had experience of galley-fight," our unknown seaman wrote, "wherein I can assure you that these four only of Her Majesty's ships will make no account of twenty galleys. There were never galleys that had better place and fitter opportunity for their advantage, but they were still forced to retire."

The sailing warship had come into her own.

2

Trouble Brewing

Trouble between England and Spain had been brewing for a long while. But it was a trouble which King Philip never came near to understanding.

In his view it was a quarrel between himself and Queen Elizabeth. She had seized the throne of England illegally. She had defied the Pope and restored the Protestant religion. She had helped Philip's Dutch subjects to revolt against him. She had sent Drake and a horde of other pirates to prey upon Spanish shipping and Spanish colonies. She was to blame for everything.

This was the way in which most princes thought in those days. A "nation" meant its ruler, not its people. "England" meant Elizabeth. "Spain" meant himself, Philip.

Rulers could intrigue and wage war against each other. They could seize each other's thrones. They could barter away whole countries, with their peoples, merely by signing a treaty, or win them by a marriage settlement. Philip had been "given" the Netherlands by his father. He had seized the throne of Portugal when it became vacant. He had thought to win England by marrying its queen.

Peoples scarcely mattered at all. Their wishes were not to be considered. Most of the peoples of Europe had become used to being shuttled about between rulers. They accepted whatever prince set himself over them. Seldom indeed had they any say in choosing him. Seldom indeed would he be a man even of their own nationality. Philip of Spain was a

The embarkation of Henry VIII at Dover, May 31st 1520.
Henry VIII had built for England the finest navy in Europe,
which his daughter Mary dismantled and laid up.

Habsburg, of mainly Austrian descent.

But England was different. Not since Norman times had a foreigner ruled in England. All later English sovereigns had been of mainly English or Anglo-Welsh stock. Almost all were native born. "I am mere English," Elizabeth boasted, and the boast was echoed by her people. They too were "mere English", and intensely conscious and proud of it. In

England this nationalism, scarcely known in the rest of Europe, was almost a religion.

It had existed in a mild way for centuries. But Elizabeth's grandfather, Henry VII, had fostered it. His task had been to heal the wounds left by the Wars of the Roses. He had taught Englishmen that they were Englishmen, not merely the followers or adherents of the houses of York or Lancaster or any other. By restoring law and order, by encouraging trade and accumulating wealth in the national treasury, he had given Englishmen an England to be proud of.

His son Henry VIII had fed this pride in a different way.

He had fought more or less successful wars. He had built for England the finest navy in Europe – fifty-three ships, great and small – plus dockyards, shore defences and a naval administration to go with it. He had lifted England's name high among the nations. And finally he had thrown off the supremacy of a foreign pope over the English church. In the process he had spent all the money accumulated by his father and had just about bankrupted the country; but most Englishmen forgave him that.

It was because of all this that they could not forgive Henry's daughter Mary. She, in their opinion, had betrayed England. She had restored the supremacy of the Pope. Worse, she had married a foreign king who thereupon claimed England as part of the Habsburg empire. Her people showed their disapproval by abusing Philip's followers in the streets. Seamen at Chatham stoned his officers when they came to inspect Henry VIII's great ships, and rioted when to please him those ships were dismantled and laid up.

They blamed Philip for that, and they blamed him and the Pope for Mary's burnings of Protestants. But most of all they blamed Philip for dragging England into a war with France in the course of which Calais was lost. It was England's last possession on the mainland of Europe. It and Dover had for two centuries past been the twin strongholds which guarded the narrow sea between England and France. It had been a main port of entry for English goods into Europe.

"Keep these two towns sure, your Majesty, as your twin eyes," an old poet had warned an English king. Now Calais was lost, in part because, of all England's once great navy, only five small ships could be mustered to defend it. To most Englishmen it was a major disaster, a supreme reason for hating Mary and her Spanish marriage.

Very little of this was understood by Philip. He knew of course that he and his Spanish followers and the marriage itself were unpopular in England. He could not help knowing that. But he did not understand that it mattered. To him the feelings of a people did not matter. He could not understand that the real trouble between England and Spain was not between Elizabeth and himself, but between the English people and him.

Even Elizabeth did not quite understand that at first. She had to learn it from her turbulent subjects.

One thing she did understand very clearly – that the treasury was empty. England could not afford a war. She had only the skeleton of a navy, no army at all, and even Henry VIII's shore defences had been allowed to decay. There was no money to put any of these things right.

At the same time either France or Spain might be tempted to attack England. The rulers of both countries laid some sort of claim to her throne – Philip through his marriage to Mary and Francis II of France because he was married to Mary Queen of Scots, great-granddaughter of Henry VII. And the Pope would probably back any such attack because of the religious question.

Elizabeth and her ministers averted that danger by playing off one country against the other. Neither France nor Spain wanted an England dominated by the other. Better an England independent and dominated by neither. Better an England ruled by the Protestant Elizabeth than by a king of France or Spain, Catholic though they both were. So Elizabeth pretended friendship alternately with France and Spain and managed to keep both nations on tenterhooks while she laboured to mend matters at home.

She succeeded in this largely by giving her people what they wanted – short of war. "I have desired to have the obedience of my subjects by love, and not by compulsion," she was later to declare.

She let them have the form of Protestant religion they wanted, though she personally would have preferred some-

OVER: *The* ROYAL PRINCE, *launched in 1610, with other ships of the period.*

thing nearer to the Catholic form – but of course without the Pope. She gave them law and order, she kept taxes to a minimum, she made parishes look after paupers and provide work for beggars, so keeping them off the roads.

She made it possible for ordinary folk to mind their own affairs, to improve their farms and businesses, to employ more workers under better conditions, and to trade overseas. So people became more prosperous. They built better houses and filled them with good furniture. Towns grew larger. Schools were set up everywhere, for even relatively poor men now wanted their children to be educated and could pay small fees.

And all this amounted to a stronger, wealthier, more prosperous nation. More prosperous in real terms than either France or Spain. Strong enough eventually to shrug off even Philip's mighty Armada.

Of all English people, the seamen were the most bitter in their hatred of Spain. And they had most cause. They were most often in contact with Spaniards.

Philip and his train of courtiers, officials and priests, had left England long before Elizabeth came to the throne. The memory of their overbearing ways and their interference in English affairs was rapidly fading from most men's minds. But seamen could not forget. They were constantly being reminded.

English seamen had to sail to Spain and, much more often, to the Spanish Netherlands. For Antwerp, in the Netherlands, was then the biggest port in Europe and a principal port of entry for British wool and cloth. In both these countries English seamen suffered annoyance and bullying by Spanish officials. Much more seriously, they ran the risk of being seized as heretics and hauled before the Inquisition. The mere possession of an English bible or prayer book could be enough to condemn a man to the galleys, or worse.

But some English seamen and the merchants they served had ambitions to trade further afield, especially to Spanish

America. It infuriated them that they were forbidden.

It infuriated them that the Pope had divided the entire world into two "spheres of influence" between Spain and Portugal. With no right at all, in English eyes, he had decreed that only Spain could explore, trade and colonise in the west, only Portugal in the east. The dividing line was roughly the meridian of 46° west longitude, or about 1,100 miles west of the Azores.

The English were not yet "a nation of shopkeepers", as Napoleon scornfully dubbed them, but trade was becoming more and more important to them. A rich merchant class was developing which was soon to become a power in the land. Just how rich they were is shown by the fact that, when the Netherlanders revolted against Spain, London merchants were able to send the rebels £500,000 out of their own pockets – a sum equal to the entire revenue of the English Crown for a year.

It must be admitted that not all English shipowners and seamen wanted merely to trade with Spain's American colonies. Many were just envious of the wealth of gold and silver which Spain was extracting from those colonies. Their ambition was simply to get their hands upon some of it, no matter how.

Nevertheless trade, more or less honest, was the dominant purpose with some, and perhaps most, until the year 1568. After that, as will be shown, English seamen virtually declared war upon Spain, whether the queen liked it or not.

3
The Traders

Prominent among the would-be traders with Spanish-America were the Hawkins family of Plymouth. Old William Hawkins, founder of the firm, had been an enterprising merchant-venturer in Henry VIII's time. Engaging with others in trade with West Africa – in defiance of the Portuguese ban – he had pushed on from there to Brazil, bringing back dyewoods for the cloth manufacturers.

Old William died in 1553, leaving his two sons, William and John, to continue the business. Both were then in their twenties. William did go to sea occasionally, but settled in the end to manage affairs ashore while his younger brother John did the voyaging.

For a while John seems to have been content with trading to Spain and Africa, but slowly his ambition grew. Why not start a regular trade with the Spanish Indies? – with, of course, the king of Spain's permission.

It seemed feasible. Elizabeth was encouraging friendship with Spain. Philip did occasionally grant licences for such trade to Italian and other merchants. And Hawkins had learnt from contacts in the Spanish-owned Canary Islands how much the American colonies needed goods of all kinds. But above all they needed slave labour, for the local Indians had proved useless for hard work and in fact were rapidly dying out.

Hawkins, from his African voyages, knew how easy it would be to obtain strong negroes cheaply, or for nothing.

*Sir John Hawkins set up the slave trade between Africa
and the Spanish Indies.*

The Portuguese were doing it all the time, either rounding
them up or buying them from local chiefs who had captured
them in tribal wars.

Hawkins went to London to get backing for the scheme.
Nobody objected. Nobody told him that slave-trading was
wicked or immoral or inhumane. Respectable, God-fearing
merchants agreed to take shares in the venture. The Queen
gave it her blessing. So Hawkins wrote hopefully to King
Philip, offering him also a share in the profits. He then went
ahead with his preparations, fitting out and provisioning three
small ships.

By the time everything was ready no reply had yet come
from Spain. Hawkins, certain that it would come in due

course, and that it would be favourable, decided not to wait for it. In October 1562 he sailed.

The voyage was entirely successful. Three hundred negroes were obtained in Sierra Leone "partly by the sword and partly by other means", as Hakluyt tells us in his *Voyages,* "besides other merchandise which that country yieldeth." All were sold openly in the West Indies and the ships loaded with "hides, ginger, sugars and some quantity of pearls." In Cuba Hawkins acquired two Spanish ships, loaded them similarly, and sent them to Seville, presumably as Philip's share.

Not until he returned to England in September 1563 did Hawkins discover that Philip's reply had been a flat refusal. He would not have "heretics" in the Indies. The two ships sent to Spain were confiscated, with their cargoes.

This was a blow; but the voyage had been so profitable that Hawkins was determined to repeat it. And this time the Queen not only approved, but offered Hawkins one of her own ships – the 700-ton *Jesus of Lubeck,* an old high-castled carrack which Henry VIII had bought from Lubeck merchants. She was not a good ship. In fact she was full of rot. But she had both guns and capacious holds. Also she looked impressive, especially when flying the Queen's standard which Elizabeth presented personally to Hawkins before he sailed. And of course the ship represented an investment by the Queen in the venture, for which she would expect a share in the profits.

It must always seem odd to us that Elizabeth, trying to keep peace with Spain, should yet lend one of her own ships for what was, in Spanish eyes, an illegal voyage. And then advertising the fact by giving Hawkins her royal standard to fly! Yet even her sister Mary had behaved in a similar way, forbidding the African trade when Portugal protested, then sending out a warship to protect it. In fact a big complaint against Mary at the time was that she could provide ships to protect an illegal trade, but not to defend Calais.

It may also seem strange that on the voyage out Hawkins

A model of the HARRY GRACE À DIEU, *flagship of
Henry VIII's great navy of fifty-three ships. It was about
a thousand tons and almost unmanageable.*

should put in at Ferrol in Spain to repair weather damage; and later at the Spanish-owned Canaries where, according to Hakluyt, the governor gave him "as gentle entertainment as if he had been his own brother".

It cannot be said that his entertainment in the West Indies was quite so brotherly. Orders had been received from Spain that local officials and settlers were to have nothing to do with the Englishmen. On the other hand the slaves and other goods were badly needed, and Hawkins was a great diplomat. By persuasion, bribery and an occasional show of force he succeeded in selling his slaves even more profitably than before. In September 1565 he was back in England, "with the loss of twenty persons in all the voyage . . . bringing home gold, silver, pearls and other jewels in great store".

This success really roused King Philip. His protest to Elizabeth was vigorous and threatening. Stop it – or else! So to calm him Elizabeth forbade Hawkins from leaving England for a year. Then probably she winked, knowing full well that Hawkins was already preparing ships for a third voyage. At any rate the preparations went ahead, and in due course the ships sailed under the command of one Captain Lovell. Hawkins stayed at home, entertaining the Spanish ambassador and trying to persuade him that he, Hawkins, was really Spain's best friend. The ships were well away at sea before the Spanish ambassador awoke to the trickery.

But this time there was little success. Hawkins said later that it was a failure "owing to the simpleness of my deputies who knew not how to handle these matters". That was putting it mildly.

In the first place Lovell obtained his slaves by seizing them from ready-loaded Portuguese ships. That brought a howl of protest from Portugal even before Lovell reached the West Indies. Hawkins had always been careful to keep out of the way of the Portuguese authorities.

And then Lovell allowed himself to be cheated at a place called Rio de la Hacha, in what is now Colombia, losing about a hundred slaves for no money at all. After which he came tamely home to report a dead loss.

It was an unimportant voyage but for one fact. One of Lovell's officers was the young Francis Drake, who had also put what money he had into the venture – and of course had lost it. He never forgave Spain. A year later he sailed into Rio de la Hacha and put a cannon shot through the governor's house. That was a little satisfaction; but it was only a trivial part of the revenge he was to take for this and a later and greater hurt.

The greater hurt was to come in 1568. When Lovell and Drake returned to England in August 1567 they found Hawkins already preparing yet another voyage. Drake, scarcely bothering to go ashore, promptly boarded Hawkins's flagship as a volunteer. Lovell, presumably, was not invited.

The flagship was to be the old *Jesus of Lubeck* once again, now expensively repaired. With her was another Queen's ship, the *Minion*. A better ship than the *Jesus*, though smaller, she nevertheless had a bad reputation. From two previous voyages she had staggered home, a floating wreck, with only a handful of her crew left alive. Seamen used to say, "The *Minion* will always come home, leaving her crew behind her." It was to prove true yet again.

Besides the Queen's ships there were four others, all smaller – *William and John, Swallow, Judith* and *Angel*. All were reckoned to be stout and efficient sailers.

Hawkins was eager to get away. Knowing the Queen, he feared she might change her mind and forbid the voyage after all. He was also afraid – so he said – that Philip might send a fleet to intercept him. That was why, when some Spanish ships were driven into Plymouth by bad weather, Hawkins opened fire on them. At any rate, that was one of his excuses.

Of course there was a tremendous row and Hawkins had to go to London to talk himself out of it. He managed to do that, but it cost him a long and unwanted delay. When the ships did at last sail, in October, food was going bad and

The JESUS OF LUBECK, *an illustration from Anthony Anthony's Roll of the Navy. It was the only ship apart from the* REVENGE *to be captured by Spain in the entire reign of Elizabeth I.*

drinking water was stinking.

Trouble dogged the voyage. A storm in the Bay of Biscay nearly sank the *Jesus* and scattered the fleet. In the Canaries some of the young gentlemen-volunteers began fighting among themselves and defying Hawkins's authority. He put a stop to that and pushed on to Africa, only to find more difficulty than ever before in getting slaves, while at the same time half his own men went down with fever and a number of others were killed in local fighting. In the end he crossed the Atlantic with only five hundred slaves instead of the thousand he had hoped to get.

On the other hand the fleet had grown, having been joined by two French Huguenot ships under a Captain

OVER: *The* WHITE BEAR, *a typical English galleon of the period.*

Bland. And, through deaths and sickness, Drake had been given command of the *Judith*.

Matters improved for a while on the coast of Venezuela. A good trade was done with only a little trouble. It was more or less completed at Rio de la Hacha where, as has been said, Drake knocked a hole in the governor's house. The governor fled, leaving the colonists to trade as they wished.

Hawkins now prepared to return home, but first he needed to repair his ships, especially the old *Jesus*. He asked for permission to do it at Cartagena, and was refused. He had to be content with obtaining firewood and fresh water and some food from a nearby island, for which – always "honest John", the peaceable trader – he left bales of English cloth as payment.

Now he had no choice but to risk the voyage home and hope to keep the *Jesus* afloat somehow. But luck was against him. Off Cuba the fleet ran into the tail end of a hurricane. The high after-castle of the *Jesus* worked loose and all her stern seams opened up. Hawkins, while his men pumped and baled furiously, had to let her run before the storm – westwards, deep into the Gulf of Mexico. All the ships followed her except the *William and John*, which made her own way home.

When the storm blew itself out Hawkins found himself within a few miles of Vera Cruz, Spain's main port in Mexico. It offered safety and repair facilities. Unlike Cartagena, it had no forts to bar his entry. On September 15, 1568, he led his ships in and moored them behind the island of San Juan de Ulua. He then discovered, to his dismay, that a large fleet was daily expected to arrive from Spain. With it was coming a new Viceroy of Mexico.

Hawkins had to accept the situation, but he prepared for the worst by fortifying the island with guns from the two big ships. The work was barely completed when the Spanish fleet arrived. And at the same time local weather-prophets predicted the coming of another storm.

Hawkins was in a quandary. His guns could keep the Spaniards outside. But then the entire fleet might be wrecked, for there was no other shelter for hundreds of miles. That would bring down on his head the wrath not only of King Philip, but of Queen Elizabeth as well. Hawkins feared Elizabeth more than Philip.

But could he trust the Spaniards? He decided he had to, if he could get some sort of guarantee. And after four days of bargaining he succeeded, getting a written agreement that the Englishmen would be left alone, with hostages held on either side for further security. So the Spanish fleet sailed in, bringing at least ten times the number of men and guns that Hawkins could muster.

And after all, Hawkins had been tricked, as Spanish documents make clear. The hostages, supposedly "gentlemen of rank", were only servants. Big Spanish ships drifted "by accident" close to the English ones. Soldiers came off to them from the town. Others gathered around the English shore batteries. Hawkins sent Robert Barrett, sailing master of the *Jesus* – who could speak Spanish – aboard the flagship to protest. He did not come back.

On September 23 one of the Spanish hostages tried to stab Hawkins at the dinner table. He failed, but at the same moment a trumpet sounded and hundreds of Spanish soldiers fell upon the Englishmen ashore and boarded the ships.

Yet the Englishmen fought back, led personally by Hawkins. Mooring ropes were cut so that the ships would drift away from the island shore. The decks were cleared of Spaniards. The guns of the *Minion* found the magazine of the Spanish flagship, which blew up. Another big ship followed her. But the English and French small ships were also sunk, except Drake's *Judith* which managed to get clear.

By nightfall the *Jesus* and *Minion* lay together in the centre of the harbour, with the *Judith* not far away, but the *Jesus* was clearly sinking. Hawkins ordered her cargo to be transferred to the *Minion*. While that was being done the Spaniards sent

Miniature of Sir Francis Drake. Drake first made a name for himself by ambushing the Spanish treasure-train outside Nombre de Dios.

fireships down. Someone hastily cut the ropes which secured the *Minion* to the *Jesus*. As the two ships drifted apart Hawkins and a few others leapt aboard the *Minion*. Young Paul Hawkins, twelve-year-old son of William Hawkins, was among those who failed to jump and were captured.

Meanwhile the little *Judith*, crammed with cargo and survivors, had got clear of the harbour. When the *Minion* did not appear next day Drake assumed she had been sunk or captured, and sailed for home. For years afterwards Drakes's enemies – and he had many among Englishmen – used to say that he had deserted Hawkins in the hour of need. But Hawkins himself never reproached him. He must have realised that Drake had done the only sensible thing.

The *Minion* was in fact sheltering behind an island while

The battle of Lepanto between Christians and Turks in 1571, showing how a sea battle was conducted when galleys were used.

her men made her more or less seaworthy. Then, desperately overloaded and short of food, she sailed painfully away from that disastrous harbour. About a hundred men, seeing starvation and death as almost certain during the long voyage ahead, asked Hawkins to set them ashore. He did so, near Tampico on the Mexican coast.

A few weeks later the *Minion* fulfilled the seamen's prophesy by limping home with only fifteen men still on their feet. William Hawkins had to send a crew out to bring her into port.

Of those who had not died ghastly tales reached England years later. Tales of torture and brutality, of slavery and whippings, of Robert Barrett, among others, burnt at the stake by the Inquisition. So the seamen of England remembered San Juan de Ulua and vowed vengeance; and especially that young firebrand, scarcely known in England and unheard of in Spain, Francis Drake.

4

The Undeclared War

"These English are great sea-dogs," wrote the Venetian ambassador, and by sea-dogs he meant pirates.

He was right. For centuries piracy had been part and parcel of English seafaring. There had been times when the men of Dover would seize a ship of Sandwich and steal her cargo, or the men of Sandwich loot a ship of Rye. Chaucer says that his 14th century "shipman" had "no nice conscience". The same might have been said of Elizabethan seamen. And not only of the seamen. Mayors and magistrates, merchants and gentry and even high officers of state sometimes financed and protected pirates and shared in their profits.

But there were degrees of piracy. It ranged from unprovoked attack, with murdering of the crew and stealing of cargo, to the mere infringement of a trading monopoly. Spain called the Hawkins trading voyages piracy.

Somewhere between came privateering, which meant getting a commission from some prince and then operating as a private warship against that prince's enemies. The French Huguenots under the Prince of Condé were at war with the Catholic king of France. The Dutch rebels under the Prince of Orange were at war with Spain. Both princes had representatives in England who would issue commissions for the asking. With a privateering commission piracy against the ships of France or Spain became, in theory, legal.

In practice privateers often attacked neutral ships as well. Their excuse, if hauled before a court to answer for it, would be that they suspected such neutral ships of carrying French or Spanish cargoes. And in practice, if privateering seamen fell into Spanish hands, they would be hanged as pirates.

For some years such pirate-privateers operated mostly in the English Channel and North Sea. But gradually, with the help of wealthy backers, they acquired better ships and turned their attention further afield, to the Azores and West Indies.

Here the French led the way. French privateers had been harrying Spain's American colonies since long before the Hawkins trading voyages began. In fact Hawkins, to get King Philip's co-operation, had once offered to chase such adventurers out of the Caribbean – an offer which Philip had indignantly rejected.

There may have been English pirates in the Caribbean before 1568, the year of the treachery at San Juan de Ulua, but if so they have left no record. What is certain is that within a year or two of that disaster at least three of Hawkins's officers were back on the coast with their own ships. One of them was Francis Drake.

Drake had no privateering commission. He asked nobody's permission, told nobody what he was about. He went, with a tiny ship of 25 tons, and came back nearly a year later. What he did nobody knows. Nobody at the time seemed to care. Francis Drake was still an unknown name. That was in 1570.

In 1571 he went out again with the same ship, *Swan*, and this time his name went into the Spanish records. "Fr. Drake, an Englishman, did rob divers barks of velvets and taffetas, besides other merchandise, besides gold and silver ..."

But he had done more than that. He had made his plans for an impudent attack on one of Spain's treasure ports – Nombre de Dios on the Isthmus of Panama. Here was collected the treasure of Peru, brought across the isthmus by mule-

OVER: *The* GRIFFIN, *a galleon of the kind that would have sailed against the Spanish Armada.*

train, for shipment to Spain. He had prepared a secret base nearby, with hidden stores. He had made friends with an outlaw tribe of Indians and runaway slaves, the Cimaroons. They had supplied him with a map of Nombre de Dios.

For this daring adventure he took out two ships, the *Swan* again, and the slightly larger *Pascha*. Their crews numbered seventy-three young men and boys – only one man was over thirty years of age. On a pitch-dark night and in pouring rain they landed from small boats at Nombre de Dios and virtually drove the Spaniards out of the town before they were properly awake. But Drake had been wounded in the leg and his trumpeter killed.

Before the massive locked doors of the King's treasure store-house Drake told his men, "I have brought you to the mouth of the treasury of the world. Now you have only to take it." Then he fainted from loss of blood. At the same time the Spaniards rallied, and someone said that the boats were already pushing off to return to the ships.

Panic followed. The men picked up Drake and ran with him to the boats, leaving the Spaniards to bury the trumpeter. The great raid had ended in fiasco.

A second attempt would be useless now that the Spaniards had been warned. But Drake produced an even bolder plan. He would waylay the next mule train as it crossed the isthmus. It meant months of waiting for the rainy season to end, and that waiting brought its troubles. Drake's younger brother John was killed in a scrap with Spaniards. Another and even younger brother, Joseph (Drake had eleven brothers in all) died of fever, as did a number of the men. When his Cimaroon friends told him that a mule-train was being prepared, only thirty of his men could stand on their feet.

He took seventeen of them, including his friend John Oxenham, and marched inland. Halfway across the isthmus came that famous moment when Drake and Oxenham climbed a tree and saw the Pacific Ocean stretched before them. Drake vowed that someday he would sail an English ship upon it, and Oxenham vowed to follow him.

But the raid itself was another failure. Something alarmed the Spaniards and they sent the treasure back. Drake and his men got nothing but the provision train – a few sacks of meal and kegs of oil.

Yet Drake refused to give up. He lay low, recruited the crew of a French privateer which happened to arrive, and made fresh plans. This time he would ambush the treasure-train on the outskirts of Nombre de Dios itself, just when its guards would be thinking all danger was over and they could relax.

And this time it worked. Within sound of the shipyards of Nombre de Dios where the homeward fleet was being prepared, they attacked the train and took from it more gold and silver and jewels than they could carry. "Our voyage is made," Drake announced. So they went home, arriving in Plymouth on a Sunday morning when everyone was at church. And the story goes that as the word went round all the congregation slipped away and down to the harbour, leaving the parson to follow if he would – which he did.

Drake had made more than a profitable voyage. He had made his name. Spain had marked him as a dangerous enemy; Elizabeth had noted him for future service. In fact for the next two years he seems to have been employed by the Queen in Ireland, though details are lacking.

Meanwhile the rush to the West Indies by other Englishmen had begun. Scores of little ships with aggressive names – *Lion, Tiger, Lion's Whelp, Dog, Wolf, Panther* – went out to hunt Spanish prey. Some were successful, some were not. Some men like John Oxenham, ended their lives on Spanish gallows, or went to the stake or the galleys. More tales of Spanish brutality reached England, keeping alive the hatred.

But some men's dreams were focussing upon a hunting-ground even further away than the Caribbean. They saw the Pacific coast of South America, practically undefended.

47

Sixteenth century seamen's dress. There was no uniform for sailors at this time, but most of them wore clothes like these – a coarse linen blouse, baggy trousers and stockings.

The idea of sending an expedition into the Pacific by way of the Straits of Magellan probably originated with Sir Richard Grenville. It was supported by Sir Christopher Hatton the banker and other merchants. John Dee, the Queen's astrologer and scientific adviser, suggested that it could do some useful exploration.

Drake seems to have heard of the project from Thomas Doughty, a gentleman-adventurer, secretary or hanger-on to Sir Christopher Hatton, who was with him in Ireland. No doubt Drake then put forward his own ideas on the subject. At any rate, when the Queen finally gave it the go-ahead, Drake was chosen to lead it, with Doughty as a kind of co-commander. As a result Grenville was furious and never forgave Drake.

John Dee the scientist had given Elizabeth the excuse she needed. The expedition, officially, was to be primarily one of exploration. Drake was to search in the far south for the supposed "lost" continent of Terra Australis; and in the far north for the equally supposed Pacific entrance to the North-west Passage. What he did between whiles was, officially, none of the Queen's business. But Drake knew very well what was privately expected of him.

Five ships set out in November 1577. The largest, *Pelican,* was of 120 tons and about 80 feet long. The smallest, *Benedict,* called a frigate, was of only 15 tons. Between them were the *Elizabeth, Marigold* and *Swan.* The crews totalled 164 men and boys.

Trouble came early. The divided command was, for Drake, impossible. Doughty seems to have intrigued for sole command, setting many of the "gentlemen" against Drake and upsetting the seamen. But the seamen were already upset. They had been told the voyage would be to Alexandria to load currants. Now they found themselves heading for the remote south of the world. Most of them would never have signed on voluntarily for such a voyage. But of course the trick had also misled Spanish spies.

Drake showed his strength when the ships anchored at Port St. Julian in Patagonia, some 200 miles north of the Straits of Magellan. Here Magellan had quelled a mutiny half a century earlier. The gibbet he had used was still to be seen, with skeletons at its feet. The cooper of the *Pelican* made wooden drinking cups from a part of it, but most men refused to use them.

Drake wanted no gibbet. He had Doughty tried for "incitement to mutiny" by a jury of forty men. He was found guilty and was beheaded – the death for a gentleman. Whether Drake was justified, whether it was a fair trial or not, has been argued about ever since.

Drake then preached his famous sermon to the assembled crews. "By the life of God, it doth take my wits from me to think of it! Here is such argument between the mariners and the gentlemen, and such stomaching between the gentlemen and the mariners, that it doth make me mad to hear it. But, my masters, I must have it left. For I must have the gentleman to haul and draw with the mariner, and the mariner with the gentleman. What, let us show ourselves to be all of a company! Let us not give occasion to the enemy to rejoice at our overthrow. I would know him that would refuse to set his hand to a rope. But I know there is not any such here!"

It was a statement of naval policy which was to echo through the centuries. It cut across class barriers. It destroyed the old idea that soldiers (as the gentlemen-volunteers mostly were) were superior to seamen. It set a pattern for the Royal Navy of the future.

The *Pelican* was now renamed *Golden Hind* in honour of Sir Christopher Hatton, whose coat of arms featured such an animal. Southward with her went the *Elizabeth* and *Marigold*, the smallest ships having been emptied and burnt. Three weeks later they were through the Straits and in the Pacific.

But that ocean was anything but pacific. Storms blew them far to the south – south of the latitude of Cape Horn, which they did not know existed. Where was the missing continent, Terra Australis? Drake decided it did not exist and, when the weather permitted, worked his way north again.

The weather was in fact appalling. In yet another storm the *Marigold* vanished with all hands. The crew of the *Elizabeth*, utterly disheartened, forced her captain to take them back through the Straits and so home.

Then at last Drake's luck returned. Fine weather came and the *Golden Hind*, alone, cruised northward along the coasts of Chile and Peru. It was almost a triumphal progress. With scarcely a hand raised against them or a shot fired her men raided one settlement after another – Valparaiso, Arica, Callao and the rest. It was, as someone said, as though a fox had been let loose in a hen run. Finally, north of the

The GOLDEN HIND. *This picture, a very small illustration from a map of c. 1590 by Hondius, is the only representation of the ship known to exist.*

Equator, they picked up an undefended galleon loaded with silver.

Drake, his "voyage made" once again, returned to the business of exploration. Pushing still northward, along the coast of California, he came upon San Francisco harbour. Was it the western end of the North-west Passage? No, it was not; but it was a fair land and he annexed it for Queen

Elizabeth under the name of New Albion. Then he decided to return home.

He chose the route across the Pacific to the East Indies – the Spice Islands. There he signed a trading treaty with a local ruler and filled what space remained in the *Hind* with cloves, which were nearly as valuable in those days as gold dust. Alas, the ship shortly afterwards struck a rock and the cloves had to be jettisoned to get her off.

Drake's chaplain, Parson Fletcher, declared the near-disaster to be God's punishment for the execution of Thomas Doughty. Whereupon Drake had him chained to the mast to cool off.

So the *Golden Hind* returned at last to Plymouth on September 26, 1580, after nearly three years. Drake's first question, to some fishermen outside the harbour, was, "Is the Queen alive and well?" It was important. If she had not been, if some pro-Spanish claimant had succeeded to the throne, Drake might have been arrested and perhaps executed. As it was he received a royal welcome and a knighthood.

He deserved it. He had achieved more than any Englishman before that time. He had "turned up a furrow about the whole world", as another Francis Drake, his nephew, later phrased it. And, of more immediate importance, he had brought back a treasure so enormous that the Queen's share alone amounted to double her annual revenue.

5
Ships and Sea Ways

Drake's voyage round the world was in fact almost a miracle. In some ways it was a greater achievement than man's first flight to the moon. Our moon explorers had a huge store of knowledge and science behind them. Every detail had been worked out and tested and tested again. Money had been poured into the project almost without end.

Drake had nothing like that behind him. Little was known of the way he had to go or the way back. The seamen prepared their ships as best they could. There was no money except what the shareholders had invested, and they expected to see a profit.

Much of the world was still unknown. Less than a hundred years had passed since Colombus had discovered America and Vasco da Gama had found the way to India. Only one ship had ever sailed right round the world – the little *Victoria*, sole survivor of Magellan's fleet.

Most of what was known was kept secret by Spain and Portugal. Log-books and charts, even private diaries and records, were classed as "top-secret". Other nations were left to glean what they could by spying or bribery.

Little was known of the means of ocean navigation, either, outside of Spain and Portugal. English seamen were expert in coastal navigation. Like Chaucer's "shipman", they "knew well all the harbours as they were, from Scotland to the cape of Finisterre." Like him, they could "reckon well the tides" and "danger all besides". Drake himself had been brought up in the coasting trade.

But ocean navigation was another matter. That involved mathematics – and mathematics, to many Elizabethans, meant just about the same thing as magic.

Portugal had its college of science at Sagres where navigation was studied and taught. Spain set up a school of navigation in Seville in 1508. France bribed away Spanish navigators to teach her pilots. But the first book describing the "new" navigation in English did not appear till 1574, and there was no proper school of navigation in England for a hundred years after that.

Drake solved the problem to some extent by conscripting a Portuguese navigator at the Cape Verde Islands. This man certainly proved his worth.

The "new" navigation meant navigating by the sun and stars. Without it, the only means of finding one's way across the ocean was by deduced or "dead" reckoning. This involved calculating or estimating as well as one could the direction and distance sailed by the ship each day, and then plotting the result on a chart. It can be done with reasonable accuracy nowadays, with modern instruments, but in those days it was haphazard.

In the first place there were no reliable charts. Some Spanish ones which Drake had acquired led him wildly astray. But not even the compass could be relied upon.

Before each reading of the compass the needle had to be rubbed with a piece of magnetic ore – the lodestone. The compass card was divided, not into 360 degrees, but into 32 points. Much worse was the fact that few seamen understood anything about magnetism. They knew that the compass did not always point to the true North Pole, but why not, and by how much it did not, were mysteries to most of them.

The speed of a ship was measured with a "log". This was simply a piece of wood attached to a line marked with knots at measured intervals. The log was tossed overboard and the line allowed to run out, the passing of the knots

Sixteenth century ships anchored in a river.

through the fingers being timed with a sand-glass. Thus so many "knots" meant a speed of so many nautical miles an hour. At the slow speeds of the ships of those days it was fairly accurate.

Much less accurate was the estimation of leeway – the sideways drift of a ship caused by the wind. This could only be guessed at.

To the ocean navigator latitude-finding by the sun or a star must have come as a great boon. But in a primitive form it had been used for centuries. Here is a priest who had been to the Holy Land in A.D. 1150 describing just how far south that country lay – "If a man lies flat on the ground, raises his knee, places his fist upon it, and then raises his thumb from his fist, he sees the Pole Star just so high and no higher."

Arab seamen crossing the Indian Ocean in their dhows measured their latitude by observing the height of the Pole Star above the horizon with a notched stick or a knotted string. Early Portuguese navigators exploring the African

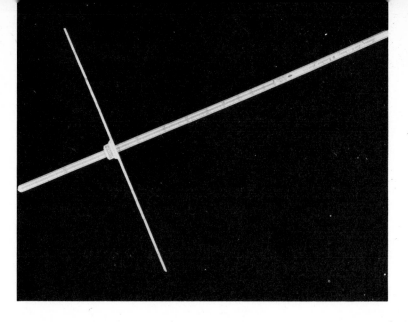

An early cross staff. This instrument was used to measure
the height of the sun or a star above the horizon.
Whenever possible, the Pole star was used to find latitude,
but it is not visible during the day or south of the equator.

coast spoke of the Pole Star as being "a lance" or "half a lance" high.

But the Pole Star can be seen only at night, when very likely the horizon is too dark to be seen. Besides which, the Pole Star cannot be seen at all in the southern hemisphere. So astronomers had to teach seamen how to use the sun instead. This was more complicated.

The Pole Star remains fairly close above the North Pole throughout the year. But in a year the sun appears to travel, between northern summer and winter, from the tropic of Cancer in the north to the tropic of Capricorn in the south, and then back – 47 degrees each way. Its exact latitude at any time – its distance from the Equator – is called its *declination*.

So astronomers had first to work out tables of the sun's declination, and then teach seamen how to use them.

To measure the altitude of the sun – its height above the horizon – most seamen used a *cross staff*. This was a graduated staff fitted with a sliding cross piece. The staff was pointed midway between the sun and the horizon, and the cross

Fireships are launched to attack the Armada sheltering in Calais. Drake has been given credit for uprooting it by this method.

An early example of an astrolabe. The astrolabe was used as an alternative to the cross staff. However, it had to be suspended absolutely vertically for a reading to be taken, which was very difficult on a rolling ship.

piece adjusted till one end appeared to touch the sun and the other to rest upon the horizon. Then the height of the sun could be read from the graduations on the staff.

But some navigators preferred to use an *astrolabe*. This was a circular plate or ring with graduations all round, and a pointer with sights for observing the sun or star. It did not measure the height above the horizon, but from a vertical datum or plumb – the result being the height of the sun or star plus 90 degrees. The disadvantage of the astrolabe was that it must be suspended absolutely vertically for a reading to be taken, which was very difficult on a rolling ship.

There was no means of finding the longitude, except by dead reckoning – calculating or estimating the distance sailed east or west. This was a problem which was to defeat even the astronomers for many years to come. Because he did not know his longitude accurately, Columbus thought he had reached the East Indies when in fact he had reached only the West Indies, which he did not know existed. Because the navigators had mis-calculated their longitude an entire

Galleys in action. When Drake attacked Cadiz the Spanish replied by sending out galleys against him as they were very manoeuvrable.
However the new English galleons were even more successful.

British fleet was wrecked on the Scilly Isles in 1707. That inspired the government to offer a big reward to anybody who could give seamen an easy means of finding their longitude at sea. The prize was won many years after that by John Harrison, the clockmaker who invented the marine chronometer.

Someone, in recent years, has called navigation "an inexact science". In Drake's day it was indeed so.

Nor were the ships exactly models of efficiency. They were very small by our standards, but that was by choice. Most explorers, pirates and even traders wanted small vessels which could be anchored in shallow rivers and bays and could be beached for cleaning or repairs. Columbus thought even his little *Santa Maria* too big, preferring the tiny *Pinta* of only 40 tons.

Such ships were seaworthy enough, in the sense that they could stay afloat in most weathers. But their tubby, round-

An early compass. Few seamen knew anything about magnetism, and although they knew that the compass did not point to the true North Pole, they did not know why.

bottomed shape made them very uncomfortable. In a rough sea they would be tossed about like corks. Their shape also made them cumbersome and difficult to handle. The biggest of them, like Henry VIII's *Harry Grâce à Dieu* and her sisters, of about 1,000 tons each, proved almost unmanageable.

Most had three masts, only the biggest having four. All the sails were square except the dhow-type "lateen" mizzen, which was triangular. There were no jibs or staysails. In place of a jib there was a small square sail beneath the bow-sprit, the spritsail. It was useful in persuading a ship to turn or in holding her to the wind, but it was nowhere near as efficient as a jib.

With this rig few ships would sail well on a beam wind, and all made a vast amount of leeway. None could point into the wind as a modern yacht will, or even as the clippers of the 19th century would. To make matters worse, the wind always caught the high poop, causing the ship to slew wildly at times.

Yet steering arrangements were crude. Wheel steering had not been invented. The rudder was controlled by a vertical lever called the *whipstaff* which passed down through the decks and was attached at its lower end to the tiller. By thrusting the lever sideways the helmsman could move the rudder, but only about five or six degrees each way.

Into a ship the size of the *Golden Hind* – about as big as a modern harbour tug – would be packed seventy or more men and everything they needed for a year or two: food and drink, powder and ammunition, ropes, timber, canvas, tar, oils and a hundred other things, not to mention cargo.

The captain had his cabin in the high poop. Below this would be the "great cabin", a communal dining saloon for the officers and gentlemen. Some parts of it might be partitioned off to form tiny sleeping cabins which even high-ranking gentlemen had to share.

The seamen lived in the fore-castle, bedding down on the bare deck or on a pile of stores. None had bunks. Hammocks, called "Spanish beds", were being used by some officers.

Very little was known of hygiene, diet or medicine. On a long voyage a big proportion of the crew always died, from typhus, scurvy and other diseases. Many were crippled by rheumatic ailments caused by exposure and wearing wet clothing for weeks on end. Nothing could be dried except by the sun and wind. No fire was permitted except for cooking. Fire was the most dreaded peril of all in these wooden ships.

Typhus was due to bad water. "Fresh" water was taken direct from any river, even from one which, like the Thames, served as a city sewer. Then the disease was spread by lice which bred on unwashed bodies and in filthy clothing and bedding. In 1589 an expedition against Lisbon lost 7,000 men from typhus and had to be abandoned.

Typhus was an epidemic, striking at random. But scurvy was inevitable. It is due to a lack of fresh food containing vitamins. It causes gums to swell and teeth to fall out. Men become weak, and then weaker still because they cannot eat, and so die. Sir Richard Hawkins, son of Sir John, reckoned that 10,000 English seamen died of it during Elizabeth's reign. He also suggested a cure – regular doses of orange or lemon juice; but it was not adopted until more than a hundred years after his death.

Seamen suffered in many other ways. They had no hospitals, no pensions, no compensation for injuries. The best a crippled seaman might expect would be a licence to beg. Pay was about ten shillings a month, or less. It was usually late in being paid and sometimes was not paid at all. If cargo was spoilt, the loss to the owner could be made good out of the seamen's wages. If a voyage was not completed, due perhaps to shipwreck, the seamen got nothing for the months already served. If a man died at sea his wife and family got nothing.

Occasionally, but very seldom, men complained. The crew of one of Drake's ships on the "beard-singeing" exploit wrote to their captain, begging him "to weigh of us like men, and let us not be spoiled for want of food, for our

*A sixteenth century globe. Maps in this period could not
be relied on. Drake used some Spanish charts that led
him wildly astray.*

allowance is so small we are not able any longer to live on
it . . . For what is a piece of beef of half a pound among four
men to dinner, or half a dried stockfish for four days in the
week, and nothing else to help withal? Yea, we have help, a
little diluted wine worse than pump water. We were pressed
by Her Majesty to have her allowance, and not to be thus
dealt withal. You make no men of us, but beasts."

For such reasons men hated and feared long voyages.
Sometimes they were tricked, as when Drake engaged his
men for a voyage to Alexandria, and then took them round
the world. More often they were impressed from trading and
fishing vessels or from the shore. "Pressing" was accepted as
the normal means of recruiting men for naval service. They
dodged it if they could. If not they went, as Sir Walter
Raleigh wrote, "with great grudging to serve in Her
Majesty's ships, as it were to be slaves in galleys".

6
Towards War

During all these years of raiding, privateering and piracy, officially there was peace between England and Spain. But open war was bound to come. Elizabeth knew it, much as she hated it. So she made ready as far as money would allow. Above all she restored the navy.

To do this she called in John Hawkins, making him treasurer of the navy and later comptroller. That gave him great power, which he used well.

One main task was to make the dockyards efficient. For years corruption in the dockyards had been a great scandal. Every official thought it his first duty to line his own pockets. High officials made fortunes. In one instance alone the Queen had paid out £7,000 for timber, receiving only £4,000 worth in return. Food was often rotten before it went aboard ship. Barrels were half empty or were filled with rubbish. Spars, ropes and canvas were of the worst possible quality. Men long dead were still, on paper, drawing their wages.

Hawkins ruthlessly sacked or punished such offenders as he could catch, and so frightened the rest that the scandal was checked – for the time being. It became even worse after he and Elizabeth were dead. So did the condition of the seamen, which in his lifetime Hawkins managed to improve. Among other things he got them a rise in pay and started a pension fund for crippled men.

But his biggest success came in the matter of the new ships which he had built, with the help of his brother William.

A Flemish carrack, a predecessor of the galleon.

When Elizabeth came to the throne the standard warship was the bluff, full-bellied, high-castled carrack. Henry VIII's celebrated *Harry Grâce à Dieu*, or *Great Harry*, may be taken as an example, though of course she was far bigger than most.

In the Mediterranean, on the other hand, the long, narrow, oared galley was still popular. From the galley was developed the galleass, somewhat higher and broader than the galley, with sails as well as oars. Neither the galley nor the galleass were of much use in the rougher northern seas. One galleass, in Henry VIII's navy, was described as "the dangerousest ship that ever men sailed in."

But from the galleass came the galleon. It appeared first in Italian waters in about 1530, but was soon adopted by Spain and Portugal. It was a full sailing ship, without oars, not quite as narrow as a galleass, but much narrower than a carrack. It was a better sailer than the carrack, but more seaworthy than the galleass.

One big weakness in the carrack had been that her high castles were added, almost as an afterthought, on top of the main hull. Consequently they were very likely to work loose and come to pieces in a rough sea. They did in the *Jesus of Lubeck*, so that, as Hawkins wrote, "We had to cut down all her higher buildings."

Another weakness was that the castles often overhung the main hull by many feet. The forecastle in particular was sometimes like a big square house, two or three storeys high, spreading right over the bows.

In the galleon both these faults were eliminated. The castles were built into the main hull. The after-castle was reduced to a long quarter-deck, with a shorter half-deck above it, and an even shorter poop-deck above that. The forecastle was similarly reduced, and was cut back so that it was entirely within the hull. Thus both structures were very much lightened, which made the ship far more sea-worthy and manageable.

A drawing by Matthew Baker showing a ship's hull designed as a fish in order to demonstrate that it must move through the water rather than float on it.

Yet these early galleons were crude compared with the new English galleons of Hawkins's navy.

Some of the designs used for the new ships, by a shipwright named Matthew Baker, still exist. This is important. It shows that at last the best builders were working from drawings. Previously, for many centuries, ships had always been built by rule of thumb and guesswork. Moreover one of Baker's drawings shows the under-water shape of a ship compared with that of a fish. It demonstrates that he at least was trying to design a ship that would go through the water easily instead of just staying afloat.

Because of this improvement in design the new ships answered their helms and generally handled far better than the old. Drake proved that by taking them into and out of

Sketch of an English galleon showing its guns. The Spanish galleons which were tall and heavy with guns were liable to topple and sink very easily if they ran into bad weather.

Cadiz. They also looked better. Queen Elizabeth, going down the Thames to name one *Repentance*, was so impressed that she changed its name there and then to *Dainty*.

But it was not only the ships which were changed. The whole conception of their use in war was also different. The old idea of a warship had always been that she must be a kind of floating fort, manned chiefly by soldiers. From her high castles soldiers would shoot down at the enemy. Then, when the sailors had put her alongside an enemy ship, the soldiers would charge out of her and fight as though on land. Spain and Portugal still thought of sea-fighting in this way.

It was no longer to be so. The cut-down and strengthened castles of the new ships carried real guns, not just soldiers with hand weapons. Below them, on the main and lower decks, were heavier guns arranged in broadsides. The intention now was that an enemy ship could be sunk or crippled by gunfire before ever the soldiers could come to grips. So for the first time there were fewer soldiers on board warships than sailors. And most of the seamen were also gunners. The seaman-gunner, who was to be the mainstay in Nelson's navy, had come into being. He was soon to prove his worth against the Armada.

After Drake's return from his world voyage events moved steadily towards open war. Spanish-backed plots to assassinate Elizabeth were discovered and foiled. So was a Spanish attempt to land an army in Ireland. But in 1584 an attempt on the life of the Prince of Orange, for which Philip had offered a reward, succeeded. Elizabeth promptly stepped up her help to the Dutch rebels and sent an army to the Netherlands.

Then in 1585 came another act of treachery by Philip. In Spain the harvest had failed. Philip invited English merchants to send all the corn they could. Scores of little ships sailed for Spain, and suddenly Philip ordered them all to be arrested and their crews seized. But one crew, of the *Primrose* of London, knocked the Spanish officials below hatches and brought them home to England, together with Philip's proclamation.

Of course there was a tremendous outcry, especially when horrifying tales began to circulate of seamen being tortured and killed by the Inquisition. Elizabeth had to take action. Drake was sent with a fleet of thirty ships – only two of which belonged to the Queen, however – to demand the release of the ships and men.

Those were his orders, but nobody thought he would be content with mere words. When it was suggested that he might use violence, the Queen shrugged her shoulders. What could she do? "The gentleman careth not if I disown him," she declared.

So he went down to Vigo in north Spain and as a beginning seized provisions and church plate. Then he went on to the Cape Verde Islands, and from there across to the West Indies, attacking, robbing and holding to ransom the two important towns of San Domingo and Cartagena. But malaria and other diseases proved worse enemies than the Spaniards. After losing 750 men he had to abandon a plan to seize the whole isthmus of Panama, and return home.

But he had done enough. He had raided the sacred soil of Spain itself. He had shown the world once again how vulnerable Spain's distant colonies were. "Truly," said Lord Burghley, "Sir Francis Drake is a fearful man to the king of Spain."

He was right, and in fact Philip had already decided that invasion of England was the only answer. He must take over the country and get rid of Elizabeth. Now that he had seized the throne of Portugal and added Portugal's navy to his own he had no doubt that he would succeed. Besides, God would be on his side. How could Francis Drake or any other heretic defy God?

Yet Francis Drake could still defy Philip, as he showed with his great "beard-singeing" raid on Cadiz in 1587. So the Armada did not set forth in that year, as all Europe had expected.

It was not Drake's Cadiz exploit alone which caused the delay. Philip himself was hesitant. Just when all seemed ready he ordered a strong squadron of galleons out to the Azores to escort the treasure fleet home. For one never knew with Drake. He might even then be out in the Atlantic waiting for them.

Then other English warships, not under Drake's command, went to the Newfoundland cod fisheries and seized the Spanish fishing fleet. So that year there would be a shortage of stockfish – dried cod – in Spain and none to spare for the Armada.

Whether the Enterprise of England would have succeeded had it been attempted in 1587 is anybody's guess. What is certain is that the year's delay, besides giving England more time to prepare, ate the heart out of the Armada.

Ships and stores deteriorated, food went rotten, men became mutinous and deserted. In the army waiting in the Netherlands, too, there was mutiny, for many men had not been paid for a year or more. They had been promised the

The Duke of Medina Sidonia portrayed as the knave of
clubs on a pack of Armada playing cards.

looting of England, but when was it to be? It was known that their commander-in-chief, the Duke of Parma, had no faith in the success of the operation, and the longer it was delayed the less he liked it.

To cap everything, Spain's great admiral the Marquis of Santa Cruz died. English seamen said it was because of his grief and anger over Drake's Cadiz raid, "that he never enjoyed a good day after." However that may be, there can be no doubt that his worries about the Armada hastened his death.

Philip had no other admiral to put in his place – at any rate, none of sufficiently high birth. So he chose the highest-ranking nobleman he could think of, the Duke of Medina Sidonia, a man who did not want the job and tried to get out of it. "I know nothing of the sea," he wrote to his king. "I am always seasick. If you send me I shall have a bad account to render of my trust." But Philip was adamant and Medina Sidonia had to go.

Even the weather seemed to be against the success of the venture. Was God really on Spain's side? In the English Channel Lord Howard of Effingham wrote, "There was never such summer seen here on the sea," and Lord Henry Seymour confirmed it. "Such summer season saw I never the like." It was the same further south. Drake, looking for the Armada in the Bay of Biscay, was driven back to Plymouth. He had heard that the Armada, which had actually sailed at last, had been driven back into Corunna.

So was there to be a respite for another year? No. King Philip had given the order. Medina Sidonia must obey. On 12 July 1588 the Armada, still weather-battered and full of seasick soldiers, finally put to sea.

OVER: *The Armada fleet sailed up the Channel in close crescent formation with transports and store ships in its rear.*

7
The Armada Comes

Was Drake really playing bowls on Plymouth Hoe when the Armada hove in sight? He may have been, but the story was not told till 1624, and then, strangely enough, it was a Spanish writer who related it.

What is certain is that on July 19 a small ship called, appropriately, *Golden Hind*, came into Plymouth under a press of sail and her master, Tom Fleming, shouted the news. The Spaniards were coming! He had seen the Armada off the Scillies. They were hard on his heels.

Drake may have stayed to finish his game, but it is unlikely. The English ships were all in harbour. A south-west breeze was blowing straight into Plymouth Sound. The ships would have to be worked out against it, perhaps to be towed by their boats – a lengthy and laborious process. There was little time to be wasted.

All that day and all night the crews worked, and by dawn the feat was accomplished. With daylight the Spaniards were amazed and horrified to see the English fleet, which they had thought to be safely bottled in port, at sea and to windward of them, in the attacking position.

Probably about fifty ships beat their way out of Plymouth that night, including a score of the Queen's galleons. The lord admiral, Howard of Effingham, was in command aboard the *Ark Royal*. His vice-admiral, Drake, was to seaward in the *Revenge*, with a squadron of twenty or so ships, big and small. Close inshore, with another squadron, was Martin

An engraving of Drake's legendary game of bowls on Plymouth Hoe.

Frobisher in the *Triumph*. John Hawkins in the *Victory*, with yet another squadron, was in the rear to cut off any retreat. Far ahead, in the Straits of Dover, Lord Henry Seymour had a reserve squadron waiting. All in all, with the small armed merchant ships which had come out from ports all along the coast, possibly more than a hundred vessels were in the chase.

Yet it was a makeshift, ill-disciplined force. Howard had difficulty in keeping his sea-dogs, including Drake, under control. Merchant skippers joined the fleet or left it just when they pleased. All thought they knew best what should be done, and often enough did it.

Matters were very different on the Spanish side. There strict discipline ruled everything and everybody. Medina Sidonia had strict orders from Philip which he dared not disobey. Every officer waited for the orders of his superior. Nobody even thought of acting on his own.

Even the ships sailed in close order, each in its appointed

place. Medina Sidonia with the main fighting force – twenty-four galleons and galleasses – led in the centre. On either wing, and slightly astern, were squadrons of powerful armed merchantmen, the great carracks and galleons of the East and West Indies fleets. In the rear, in the hollow of this widespread crescent formation, were the transports and storeships. The total fleet comprised well over a hundred ships, of which possibly sixty might be called warships.

It was a good formation. As long as it held the English ships could do little against it except snipe at its wings. But Lord Howard was quite content to do this for the time being. His main job, as he saw it, was to prevent the Spaniards from making a landing.

He considered all the possibilities. If he had been Medina Sidonia, he would have wanted early on to seize some western port, to cover the way back to Spain. Plymouth seemed a likely target. So for the first day or two Howard kept much of his force back, guarding Plymouth. But the Armada swept steadily on.

Where then? Torbay? Portland? The Isle of Wight? Each seemed possible, so each had to be guarded in turn. But the Armada still swept on.

Howard would have been easier in his mind had he known that Medina Sidonia had no choice in the matter. His orders from Philip were that he must not attempt a landing till he reached the Thames estuary, where Parma's army from the Netherlands would join him. But Howard did not know that.

There were moments of excitement. On July 21 a big Spanish ship, the *San Salvador*, blew up, apparently by accident. Then two other big ships collided and one of them, badly damaged, drifted astern of the fleet. That night Drake came upon her, finding an enormous treasure on board, and sent her into port under escort. That infuriated Frobisher, who declared, "We will have our shares, or I will make him spend the best blood in his body!"

The same night Howard in the *Ark Royal* pressed on too

*Howard of Effingham was commander-in-chief of the
English fleet that went out to meet the Spanish Armada.
Drake was his second-in-command.*

hard and found himself almost surrounded by Spanish ships
in the hollow of the crescent, and had to fight his way out.
Next day Frobisher, working inshore to prevent a possible
landing on Portland, got separated from the main English
fleet by a strong squadron of Spaniards. He was rescued from
that situation by Drake, sweeping in from seaward, which
must have annoyed the peppery Frobisher still more.

As each danger point was reached Howard attacked – off
Portland, the Isle of Wight, Selsey Bill. Little visible damage
was done and no ships were sunk. But the effect of this con-
tinual harrying upon the Spaniards was demoralising. Worse
still, they were rapidly using up their stocks of ammunition
and powder. The English could replenish theirs from the
shore, and did so time and again. But for the Spaniards there
was no such relief, unless perhaps they could get it from
France.

That was possibly one reason why, after passing Selsey, Medina Sidonia took the Armada across the Channel and anchored it, on July 27, in Calais Roads. Another reason was that he *must* get in touch with the Duke of Parma, from whom no word had come. Was the army of the Netherlands ready for the invasion? Where was it? Medina Sidonia sent as messenger an illegitimate son of King Philip, galloping overland, to demand an answer.

In fact the army was not ready. Unpaid and mutinous, it was encamped many miles from the sea.

Whether the English admirals knew that or not, they did know that the Armada must be given no respite. But how was it to be uprooted from Calais? Drake is supposed to have given the answer – fireships.

A Spanish officer wrote, "We rode there all night, with a great foreboding of evil from that devilish people and their arts." And at two in the morning his foreboding was justified. That cry went up which was perhaps most dreaded of all in those days of wooden ships. "Fireships!"

They came in with a rising wind and a strong tide, eight small ships filled with oils, pitch, tallow and powder. Spanish nerves, already frayed, now broke completely. Panic-stricken men rushed to cut cables and hoist sails. Some ships collided. A great galleass lost her rudder and, rowed by three hundred slaves, rushed headlong on to the beach, a swarm of English pinnaces after her. But most ships went where the wind took them, into the North Sea.

They were in no sort of order now. The great crescent formation which had been the Armada's strength was broken for ever. Medina Sidonia tried desperately to form some sort of line, but it was hopeless. Off Dunkirk, where Parma's army should have been waiting, he rallied a few ships and turned back bravely to meet the assault of Drake, Hawkins and Frobisher. Miles inland, on the road in his coach, the

OVER: *The* ARK ROYAL, *Howard of Effingham's flagship.*

Duke of Parma heard the thunder of the guns. He did not yet know that the great invasion was already an exploded dream.

Battered and leaking, desperately short of powder and shot, the Spanish ships turned again and fled. Dutch ships came out to join in the chase. Two Spanish ships fell into their hands at once, though one sank. Only a change of wind saved others from driving ashore in the shallows of the coast of Holland.

Howard, concerned still about the possibility of invasion, now worried about the chance of a landing in Scotland. So he kept up the chase, though by this time some of the English ships were in no better condition than their enemies. Drake's *Revenge*, as someone reported, "was shot as full of holes as a colander". Some ships had no powder left. Food was scarce, or rotten. Worst of all, typhus was raging in the fleet.

At last, off the Scottish coast, the chase was called off. The weather, getting worse all the time, could be left to take care of the remnants of the Armada. And it did. "God breathed and they were scattered," as Elizabeth had inscribed on medals after the event. The great ships laid their bones around Scotland and Ireland. Thirty-five vanished completely. Thousands of men were drowned, hundreds were killed when they struggled ashore in Ireland. Yet about forty ships did eventually get back to Spain, mere floating wrecks manned by skeleton crews.

Against that the English had lost no ships, and only about a hundred men had died by enemy action. But typhus killed far more. They lay in the streets of seaside towns because householders, terrified of the disease, would not take them in. "The best lodging I can get for them," wrote Howard from Margate, "is barns and outhouses." He refused to go to London for the victory celebrations, but joined Hawkins in doing what he could for the seamen, including seizing some of the treasure which Drake had found aboard his Spanish prize, to buy food and medicine.

*Drake's dial. Drake had it made for his expedition to the
West Indies in 1570. It has a compass, tables of latitude,
and tides, and a quadrant for measuring angles and
heights in observing the sky.*

The Armada medal struck to commemorate England's victory.

8

The Sunset Years

The defeat of the Armada did not mean the total defeat of Spain. It did not mean even the end of attempts at invasion. Yet it did have lasting effects. It taught England the value of her navy, and that her future power must lie upon the sea. It taught her, and the rest of Europe, that Spain was not invincible – that even her most determined efforts could be brought to nothing. In that sense it did indeed mark the beginning of the end of Spanish power.

But in the shorter term is also benefited Spain. It taught her a lesson in naval warfare. It taught her the value of possessing command of the sea, of the ability to protect her sea routes and her distant colonies.

Within a year or two Spain had galleons fully as efficient as England's. They were built, sad to say, with the help of renegade English shipwrights. Their seaworthiness was improved, and their gunnery. They were at least partly responsible for the relative failure of English operations after 1588, in the sunset years of Elizabeth's reign.

Only nine months after the defeat of the great Armada Elizabeth attempted a similar operation in reverse. Its purpose was to land an army in Portugal to seize the throne of that country for one Don Antonio, a cousin of Philip's. An unwieldy fleet of 150 vessels set out carrying 10,000 soldiers. Drake commanded the fleet, Sir John Norreys the army. Both men, hoping to make a profit, had invested money in the venture.

Alas, it was a complete failure. Drake, disobeying orders, insisted upon raiding Corunna first. That achieved nothing except the capture of a vast amount of wine, upon which sailors and soldiers alike got roaring drunk and remained so for a week. Then, when the main assault on Lisbon came to be made, the army discovered that it had no siege guns. Nor could it get any help from the fleet, for the big ships were unable to work their way up the River Tagus because of a foul wind.

Everything else went wrong. The Portuguese people did not rise in support of Don Antonio, as he had promised they would. Typhus broke out and, as usual, struck down far more men than did the enemy. Dismally the stricken army retired to the coast and re-embarked. Drake, who had hoped to go on afterwards to raid the Azores, was forced to carry the remnant back to England. Elizabeth, in a towering rage, blamed Drake for the failure.

Drake was not alone in seeing the Azores as a weak joint in Spain's armour. All Spanish treasure ships coming home from the West Indies called there. Yet the islands were difficult to defend from Spain, while being close enough to England to be raided. Hawkins and some others had for years advocated the maintenance more or less permanently of an English squadron in Azorean waters.

Not until 1591 was any attempt made to follow this policy, and by then it was too late. Spain had seen the danger and was ready to combat it. All treasure ships, in future, were to be met at the Azores by a substantial fleet and escorted home.

The English squadron which set out in 1591 was commanded by Lord Thomas Howard, a relative of Howard of Effingham. Drake, in disgrace because of the Lisbon failure, was deliberately excluded. And to rub salt into his wounds the command of his old flagship *Revenge* was given to one of his bitter rivals, Sir Richard Grenville. Thus it was with Grenville's name, not Drake's, that the *Revenge* passed immortally

Martin Frobisher commanded a squadron in the English fleet against the Armada. His peppery disposition quickly led to arguments with Drake.

into English naval history.

Bad weather, disease and shortage of food forced the squadron to seek shelter and refreshment in a bay in one of the islands. Hundreds of sick men were put ashore and some ships were partially dismantled for refitting. And at that moment a huge fleet of warships from Spain arrived.

Howard immediately ordered the squadron to sea, in whatever state they might be. Grenville, perhaps from sheer obstinacy, perhaps because he simply had not sufficient men on board to work the ship, or perhaps – as Sir Walter Raleigh preferred to believe – because he would not leave his sick men to be captured, kept the *Revenge* back until all were on board. As a result the Spanish fleet was able to cut the *Revenge* off from the rest of the English squadron.

Grenville had one slim chance of escape, by setting all sail and running before the wind in the only direction still open to him. "But," says Sir Walter Raleigh, "Sir Richard utterly refused to turn from the enemy, alleging that he would rather choose to die than dishonour himself and her Majesty's ship." So with crazy bravery, and to the dismay of his crew, he set the *Revenge* straight for the Spaniards, to try to force her way out between them.

So astonished were the Spaniards that some ships actually did give way to the English galleon, and for a short while it looked as though Grenville's effrontery might succeed. But then the huge *San Philip*, twice as big as the *Revenge*, blundered into the English ship's vicinity and cut off the wind from her sails. Immediately four or five other Spaniards closed in and the fight was really on.

The Spaniards had copied the English galleons, but perhaps not until this moment did they appreciate fully their fighting power. A single broadside from the *Revenge* caused such havoc to the *San Philip* that she had to retire, and some said that she sank. Certainly two other ships were sunk and at least fifteen at various times were beaten off with heavy loss.

All afternoon the fight went on, all evening and through the night. Time and again attempts were made to board the *Revenge*, each time to be beaten back. But by morning it was obvious that the end must be near. As Raleigh's account says, "All the powder of the *Revenge* to the last barrel was spent, all her pikes broken, forty of her best men slain and the most part of the rest hurt . . . There remained no comfort at all, no hope. The masts were all beaten overboard, all her tackle cut asunder, her upperworks razed, and in effect evened she was with the water, nothing but the very foundation or bottom of a ship."

Grenville himself had been seriously wounded, but refused to leave the deck. Instead he ordered the gunner to use that last barrel of powder to sink the ship so that "the Spaniards should never glory to have taken one ship of her Majesty's."

The gunner, whatever his own inclination might have been, was not allowed to obey. He was seized, while another

Sir Walter Raleigh wrote a vivid account of Grenville's brave last fight in the REVENGE.

officer slipped away to make terms with the Spanish admiral. So the battered *Revenge* was at last surrendered and Sir Richard Grenville, a dying man, was taken aboard the Spanish flagship. Weakly he told them "that they might do with his body what they listed, for he esteemed it not."

In fact he died a few days later, and soon after that a storm sank the *Revenge* with her Spanish prize crew on board. Fourteen Spanish ships went down with her. As Raleigh summed it up, "So it pleased them to honour the burial of the renowned ship *Revenge*, not suffering her to perish alone, for the great honour she received in her lifetime."

In the whole of Elizabeth's long reign only two of her warships fell into enemy hands. One was the *Revenge*, which sank. The other was the old *Jesus of Lubeck*, abandoned at Vera Cruz in 1569, which was sold for scrap.

So the war dragged on, with small profit to either side, and considerable expense. To Elizabeth of course, the expense was more important than to Philip. If Spanish treasure ships could have been captured she might have been consoled, but such achievements now were rare indeed. Drake had failed. Thomas Howard had failed and had lost the *Revenge*. Hawkins made a long cruise off the Portuguese coast and also failed, so he joined Drake in disgrace. Only Martin Frobisher had any outstanding success, bringing home a rich prize in 1592. For that he was promoted to the Queen's favour, becoming for a while her chief naval adviser.

His triumph over his old rival Drake was to be short-lived. In 1594 he was sent to Brest with a fleet and an army under Sir Thomas Baskerville to relieve the French Huguenots besieged there. The attempt was successful, but Frobisher, leading an assault party, was killed.

Whether she would or not, Elizabeth had now to turn again to Drake and Hawkins. Between them they urged her to make a full-scale assault upon the source of Spain's treasure, the West Indies and Central America. Get at the treasure before it is shipped, they advised. Why wait for the chance of picking up ships at sea?

It might have been successful if it had been efficiently carried out, and at once, but it was not. To begin with *both* Drake and Hawkins were appointed to command it, with Sir Thomas Baskerville, the hero of Brest, in charge of 2,500 soldiers. A divided command is seldom effective, and in this case it must almost certainly lead to trouble. Drake and Hawkins were men of entirely different temperaments. Drake was dashing; Hawkins cautious. Drake, now in his fifties, was so self-confident that he would listen to no advice and often refused to take the most elementary precautions. By contrast Hawkins, in his sixties, had become so slow that "his meat grew cold before it reached his mouth."

Sir Richard Grenville who commanded the REVENGE,
one of only two English ships to fall into Spanish hands
in Elizabeth I's reign. The REVENGE *sank in a storm*
and Grenville died of his wounds.

Secondly, just as the fleet was ready to sail in the spring of
1595, rumours came of the preparation of a second Spanish
Armada. Elizabeth thereupon cancelled sailing orders and
sent Baskerville off to inspect coastal defences. It was not until
the end of August that Elizabeth finally gave permission for
the voyage to commence.

The delay had been fatal. News of the venture had reached
Spain and all colonial governors had been warned. And in the
fleet thousands of idle and disgruntled men had been eating
their way through the stores intended for the voyage.

Four days out from home Drake announced that his ship
was already short of food, in part because he had shipped
three hundred more men than had been allowed for. Could
Hawkins help out? Hawkins was furious and refused. Drake
retorted that it would therefore be necessary to call at the

Carracks and galleasses were both predecessors of the galleon, but were by comparison cumbersome and difficult to manoeuvre, especially in bad weather.

Canary Islands, instead of proceeding directly to the West Indies as had been intended. Hawkins refused again, but eventually Baskerville the soldier persuaded him to agree.

It was by that time obvious that the treasure ships for that year would have been loaded and must be well on their way home. But a report had come of one ship, exceptionally valuable, being delayed at San Juan in Puerto Rico. Hopes were pinned on that. First this call at the Canary Islands must be made.

It brought only more trouble. Drake was all for a direct assault on the chief town, Las Palmas. Baskerville, seeing a vicious surf breaking on the beaches, a line of forts and a small army waiting, refused to let his men go. Angrily Drake attempted a landing with the seamen, only to be driven back by a storm of shot. Ignominiously the fleet had to retire to another island. Perhaps they could get fresh water and steal a few goats.

The fact was that times had changed. Even the herds of goats were guarded now. Some of the men sent to seize them were captured by soldiers and, perhaps under torture or the threat of it, told the Spaniards where the fleet was bound. Promptly a fast frigate was despatched to warn the governor of Puerto Rico.

So it was November before the already distressed fleet came in sight of Puerto Rico. And as it did so that once-great man, Sir John Hawkins, died. He it was who had shown Englishmen the way to the riches of the New World. He it was who, perhaps more than any other Englishman, had ensured the defeat of the great Armada and his country's survival. Now, alone and unmarked, he was committed to the sea which had brought him both triumph and disaster.

Now in sole command, Drake acted typically. He led his ships into the harbour, anchored in full view of the forts, and went to dinner. But times had indeed changed. Scarcely had he sat down when a cannon-ball tore through the cabin and killed two officers sitting with him. Once again the ships were compelled to withdraw ignominiously and seek a safer berth.

A night attack with boats was no more successful. It cost the lives of fifty men with fifty more wounded, but produced no loot worth having. Baskerville reconnoitred inland, but decided that a landward assault was not worth making. The place was altogether too well defended. "I will bring you to twenty places more wealthy and easier to be gotten," Drake promised him airily, and so Puerto Rico was left.

But the places to which Drake now led the fleet were, though easy to take, scarcely more rewarding. First, Rio de la Hacha, against which he seemed to nourish a permanent grudge. It was empty of citizens and goods. So was Rancheria, not far away, where once had been a flourishing pearl fishery. Ah, said Drake, but these places were only stepping stones on the way to Nombre de Dios. What treasure they would find there!

They did not. Unknown to Drake, Nombre de Dios had long ago been deserted by the Spaniards in favour of a new port, Puerto Bello, some twenty miles away. They found a ghost town, with empty houses and grass-grown streets.

Even then undaunted, Drake instructed Baskerville how to cross the Isthmus to Panama, where he would find the treasure of Peru waiting. But his instructions were yet again years out of date. The old trail had been abandoned and the jungle had closed over it. A new highway had been made from Puerto Bello, with a string of forts to guard it. Baskerville struggled on with his inexperienced, sick and disheartened men, until an Indian they captured told them that Panama was well defended and, worse, knew of their approach. It would be almost impossible to take the town.

It was said of Drake that when he saw Baskerville's ragged and downcast men returning he "never again carried mirth nor joy in his face". Yet he could still pretend that all would be well in the end. They must go to this new port, Puerto Bello. But even if that failed, there were so many other places.

*Drake's body is buried at sea. In 1595 Drake and
Hawkins made their last voyage to the West Indies. Both
died at sea in the course of it.*

All must be well.

The truth was that he was ill. As the fleet struggled against
head winds to reach Puerto Bello he "began to keep his
cabin", which no man had known him do before. On the
night of January 27 he began to rave, using strong language
"that no-one cared to record". Early next morning, after
trying to get into his half-armour so that he could meet his
end like a soldier, as he said, he died. So he too was committed
to an unmarked grave in the sea which had brought him so
much fame and honour.

His men burnt Puerto Bello, but it gave them little satisfaction. There was no treasure to be had. The citizens had
fled, taking even their household goods with them. And that
was practically the end of the adventure. Baskerville, the
soldier, took the fleet home. Ironically, the only success of
the voyage came to him, for off Cuba he met a Spanish fleet
and defeated it.

Ironically, too, when the survivors reached home they
found that Elizabeth had been right in hesitating to let it sail.

A second Spanish armada *was* being prepared. With no profit coming from the West Indies venture, she yet had to meet this new threat.

But meet it she did, by taking a leaf out of Drake's book and sending a fleet – and an army – to Cadiz. Howard of Effingham took the fleet, the young Earl of Essex the army. And for once all went well. Cadiz was captured and an immense quantity of shipping and stores seized or destroyed. It was Drake's "singeing of the king of Spain's beard" over again, except that Drake had used only a small squadron of ships and no soldiers. At any rate Elizabeth was well pleased and gave Howard of Effingham an earldom by way of reward.

Yet, as with Drake's earlier exploit, the sailing of the armada was only delayed, not prevented altogether. With ninety ships and possibly 10,000 soldiers it put to sea late in the summer, only to be wrecked in a storm off Cape Finisterre. Such of its men as survived promptly deserted.

A less dedicated man than Philip of Spain must have doubted by this time whether God was indeed on his side. But Philip seems to have had no doubt on that score. A year later, in 1597, yet another armada sailed, his third, and yet again a storm destroyed it. Whether he would have tried again we do not know, for in 1598 he died. Certainly his successor, Philip III, did make one more attempt, in 1601. But it was a half-hearted effort. A relatively small fleet succeeded in landing some 4,000 seasick men in Ireland. The Irish Catholics gave them little support. Elizabeth's troops easily defeated them, while her navy cut off their escape. The much-vaunted Enterprise of England had reached its end at last.

Yet the war itself lingered on; or, rather, there was not yet official peace. In the early days there had been official peace between England and Spain, but in reality a state of war. Now the reverse was true. There was no peace, yet there were few acts of war. Except, of course, that private warships were still active. There was no safety yet for Spanish shipping in the Channel, while in the West Indies small English,

Drake's drum. Legend said that if this drum were ever sounded Drake would return to help England in her hour of need.

French and Dutch vessels still pecked away at Spanish colonial trade.

It had to come to an end, and it did. Elizabeth died in 1603. Her successor, James I, son of Mary Queen of Scots, sent Howard of Effingham to Spain to negotiate terms of peace.

It was yet another irony that he, who had led the seamen of England in the greatest defence of their country ever made to that date, should bring back terms which most of them regarded as a betrayal. Spain was to regain all she had lost. English ships were forbidden to trade with the Spanish colonies. All privateering commissions were cancelled and all privateers at sea automatically became pirates. The splendid galleons which had saved England were to be laid up, their seamen turned loose to beg or starve. They were forbidden even to seek service in foreign ships. It was peace at any price, and the price was shameful.

So the navy of Elizabeth, of Hawkins and Drake and the rest, was destroyed. It was not to be revived in any strength for nearly fifty years.

Acknowledgements

THE BRITISH TOURIST AUTHORITY 93

MAGDALEN COLLEGE Cambridge 35, 67

THE MANSELL COLLECTION 51

NATIONAL MARITIME MUSEUM London 12, opp. p. 16, 17, 22, 26–27, 31, 36–37, between p. 40 & 41, 44–45, 55, between p. 56 & 57, 56, 57, 60, 63, 68, 71, between p. 71 & 72 (and front jacket), 78–79, 81, 84, between p. 88 & 89

NATIONAL MARITIME MUSEUM: Greenwich Hospital Collection 76

NATIONAL PORTRAIT GALLERY 10, 11, 85, 88

RADIO TIMES HULTON PICTURE LIBRARY 91

THE SCIENCE MUSEUM 15, opp. p. 33, 58–59, 65

WAYLAND PICTURE LIBRARY 48, 74

COLLECTION OF THE DUKE OF BEDFORD Woburn Abbey (photograph by John Webb): back jacket, frontispiece

Index

Page numbers in italics refer to pictures. Those marked with an asterisk★ refer to plates that fall between or opposite these pages.

A

Accommodation in Tudor ships 61
After-castle 38, 66
Angel 34
Antonio, Don 82, 83
Ark Royal 73, 75, *78–79*
Armada 14, *16*★, 17, 20, 28, *56–57*★, *70*, *71*, *72*★, 73–80, 82
Astrolabe 57
Astronomical navigation 54
Azores 29, 83–86

B

Baker, Matthew 67
Baskerville, Sir Thomas 87–91
Benedict 49
Borough, Admiral William 16, 18–19
Burghley, Lord 70

C

Cabin 61
Cadiz 14–20, *58–59*, 70, 92
Calais 24, 32, 76
Canary Islands 89
Carrack 14, 16, 19, 32, *65*, 66, 75, *88–89*★
Cartagena 38, 69
Charts 54
Cimaroons 46
Columbus, Christopher 53, 57, 60
Compass 54, *60*
Condé, Prince of 42
Conditions in Tudor ships 62
Cross staff *56*, 57
Cuba 32, 91

D

Dainty 68
Declination of sun 56
Deduced or "dead" reckoning 54
Dee, John 48, 49
Despatch boat 14
Diseases of seamen 62
Dog 47
Doughty, Thomas 48, 49
Drake, Sir Francis *8–9*, 11, 15, *16*★, 18–21, 34, 38–39, *40*, 41, 43, 46–54, *56–57*★, *58–59*, 62, *63*, 67–70, 72–74, 76–77, 80, 82–83, 87–90, *91*, 92, 93
Drake, Francis (the second) 52
Dreadnought 16

E

Elizabeth 49–50
Elizabeth Bonaventure 16, 18–19
Elizabeth I, Queen of England 10–11, 21–22, 23, 25, 28, 30–34, 39, 47–49, 52, 64, 68–70, 80, 82, 83, 86–88, 91–93
"Enterprise of England" 14, 73–80, 92
Essex, Earl of 92

F

Fireship 18, 40, *56–57*★, 77
Flagship 16, 18–19
Flyboat 18
Forecastle 61, 66
Frigate 49, 89
Frobisher, Sir Martin 74, 76, 77, *84*, 87

G

Galleass 14, 66, 77, *88–89*★
Galleon 17–20, 66–67
Galley 17–20, *40–41*★, *58–59*, 66
Gama, Vasco da 53
Golden Hind 73
Golden Hind ex *Pelican* 16, 50, *51*, 52
Grenville, Sir Richard 48, 83–86, *88*
Griffin 44–45
Guns and gunnery 68–69

H

Hakluyt 32–33
Half-deck 66
Harry Grace à Dieu (Great Harry) 32★, 61, 66
Hatton, Sir Christopher 48
Hawkins, Sir John 11, 30–35, 38–43, 64–67, 74, 77, 80, 83, 87–89, 90–91
Hawkins, William (the elder) 30
Hawkins, William (the younger) 30, 40–41, 64
Henry VII, King of England 23, 25
Henry VIII, King of England *22*, 23–25, 30, *32*★, 61, 66
Howard of Effingham, Lord 72–73, 75, *76*, *78–79*, 80, 92
Howard, Lord Thomas 83–84, 87
Hulk 14

I

Impressment of seamen 63

J

James I, King of England 93
Jesus of Lubeck 32, 34, *35*, 38–39, 66, 87
Judith 34, 38–40

K

Knot 54–55

L

Latitude 55–56
Leeway 55–56
Lion 16, 19, 47
Lion's Whelp 47
Lisbon 14, 83
Lodestone 54
Log 54
Longitude 57, 60
Lovell, Captain 33–34

M

Magellan, Ferdinand 49
Magellan, Straits of 50, 53
Magnetism 54
Marigold 49–50
Mary I, Queen of England 7, 10, *11*, 24, 32
Mary Queen of Scots 25, 93
Medina Sidonia, Duke of *71*, 72, 74–76
Minion 34, 39–41

N

Napoleon 29
Navigation 53–58, 60
Nelson 68
Newfoundland cod fisheries 70
Nombre de Dios 14, 15, 43, 46–47, 90
Norreys, Sir John 82
North-west Passage 49, 51

O

Orange, Prince of 42, 69
Oxenham, John 46–47

P

Panama 15, 43–47, 90
Panther 47
Parma, Duke of 72, 75, 77, 80
Pascha 46
Pelican 49–50
Philip II, King of Spain 7, *10*, 11, 14, 18, 21, 24–25, 28, 31–34, 39, 43, 69–70, 72, 74, 87, 92
Philip III, King of Spain 92
Pinnace 14, 77
Pinta 60
Pirates and piracy 11, 42–43
Pole star 55–56
Poop-deck 61, 66
Primrose 69
Privateers 42–43
Puerto Bello 90
Puerto Rico 89

Q

Quarter-deck 66

R

Rainbow 16
Raleigh, Sir Walter 63, 84, *86*
Repentance 68
Revenge 73, 80, 83–87, *88*
Royal Prince 26–27
Rio de la Hacha 33, 34, 38, 90

S

Sails 61
San Juan de Ulua 38–41
San Philip 85
San Salvador 75
Santa Cruz, Marquis of 19, 72
Santa Maria 60
Scurvy 62
Seymour, Lord Henry 72, 74
Slave trade 30–40
Spice Islands 52
Steering gear 61
Swallow 34
Swan 43, 46, 49

T

Terra Australis 49, 50
Tiger 47
Triumph 74
Typhus 62, 80, 83

V

Vera Cruz 38
Victoria 53
Victory 74

W

White Bear 36–37
William & John 34, 38
Wolf 47